ISBN 978-0-9509366-0-4

Printed by Beaverprint, Gloucester

INTRODUCTION

SĀNDOR PETÖFI was born on January 1st 1825.
He died in battle on July 31st, 1849 at SEGESVĀR
leading the revolution against Hapsburgian oppression.
The 26 years of his life were full of violence, hate, love,
triumph and defeat.
He had been an actor, soldier and tramp.

PETÖFI has been described as:-
The greatest Hungarian poet.
A man of the people.
A spokesman for the poor and underprivileged.
A burning, restless soul.
A patriot and prophet.
A comet, drawing a fiery trail across the heavens,
vanishing suddenly.
He was inspired by the idea of world liberty.
His fictional 'APOSTLE' richly contains the contrasts
of tragedy, joy, love and hate, within the confines of
poverty and injustice.

Translated from the Hungarian
by JOAN NEININGER.

PART ONE

Dark is the town, as skies
are overhung by night.
The moon has gone adventuring
in other regions bright.
The stars have closed their golden eyes,
and so black is the world, it lies
like conscience, leased outright.

But one small light
is shining high,
of weakness dying,
like the meditative eye
of an invalid,
one final hope espying.

It is an attic's pale nightlight.
Who sits beside this floating wick?
Who's keeping watch tonight?
Two brothers do this vigil share:
Poverty and Virtue!

Great is the poverty in here,
within this room so small,
that there is hardly room at all.
This attic, like a swallow's nest,
and yet not more ornately dressed.
Bleak, with all the four walls bare,
excepting for the trimmings
created by the mildew.
And streaked with stains
where run the rains,

which seep the attic through . . .
These traces,
thickly by the rain outlined,
are like a bell-cord intertwined,
such as are hung in wealthy places.
The atmosphere is so depressing,
from breathing sighs, and the oppressing
smell of mouldiness!
The landlord's dogs, although accustomed to the farm,
would possibly have perished, were they here.

A pinewood bed, and pinewood table,
worthless on the second-hand market.
At the foot of the bed,
is an old straw mattress, and a pair
of rush-seated chairs by the table there.
Laid to rest, at the head of the bed,
is a worm-eaten chest.
That is all the furniture
of which this room is blest.

Who are the people living here?
Beside the lamp, now flickering
and tiring, from bickering
with the darkness and the light . . .
the varied forms emerging
from half-shadow into sight,
like faded dreams appear.

Does the attic's light deceive the eye?
Why are they beneath this roof,
so ashen grey?

Or can the reason be that the inhabitants I see,
are ghosts, materialising in this way?
This poor, poor family!

Sitting there upon the chest,
with her baby at her breast, is the mother.
Unhappy little suckling child!
Amid stifled sobs, it rests awhile,
from sucking wildly at the arid breast in vain.
The woman's sitting pensively,
with thoughts which are apparently charged with pain.
Like thawing snow beneath the eaves,
brimming tears are shed.
They trickle slowly down her face,
and drop upon the baby's head . . .
Or perhaps there is no thought at all.
And from her eyes, tears only fall
from custom now, unconsciously,
which like the stream, oblivious of it's flow,
downward from the rocky peak,
runs naturally so?

Thank goodness the eldest child's asleep.
(Unless it only seems he's sleeping?)
Within the bed, beside the wall,
and overspread with coarse sheeting,
from which below, the straw is peeping.
Sleep, little boy.
And may the dry bread of your dreams,
be transformed within your hand,
into an apple, royal and red!

The father, a young man, with darkened brow,
is sitting by the table . . .
From this brow, perhaps has come
the gloom which permeates the room?
His brow, a book in which the world
has written all it's care,
a picture which portrays
life's sorrow in a million ways.
But underneath the forehead dark,
are two bright eyes which flare and spark
like meteors, darting everywhere,
without fear of anyone,
and yet which everybody fears.
Always he is in aspiration
of what is above and beyond
man's immediate comprehension.
Unconfined by earthly shrouds,
he soars into the infinite,
like an eagle among clouds!

PART TWO.

The great world, in outer silence sleeps.
The inner silence, the small room keeps.
There is only an occasional sigh
of the autumn breeze without,
and the other occasional sighing within,
of the mother.

The little boy quietly sits up in bed,
with his back to the wall,
weakly leaning his head.
In sepulchral whispered entreaty, he said:

4

"Father, I'm hungry!
I try and try, but cannot sleep;
My hunger hurts me so.
Oh Father, give me bread,
or do but show it unto me.
That even would be good
if the bread I were to see."

"Wait until tomorrow, my dear son.
Wait until tomorrow for your bread.
You shall have a white loaf, with roasted cockerel,
if you wait until tomorrow little one."

"But Father,
I would rather have stale brown bread today,
than a white new loaf tomorrow,
for by the morrow, I could die,
and I know that I would die ....
It's such a long time coming,
that tomorrow which you speak of,
and it always is today, still this day
on which I cry for hunger, everyday!
Father, I do wonder whether when we die,
and in the grave together lie,
shall we be hungry then?"

"No, my child,
we shall no longer hunger,
when we die."

"In that case, I shall wish for death.
Please get for me a coffin,
one as white as Mother's face,

and small, to put me in.
Take me to the cemetery,
below the ground, to bury me.
So happy now, must be the dead,
to hunger nevermore for bread!"

Who would say children are innocent?
Where is the dagger or sword to be found
that could torture yet greviously more?
What blade could impart
such a wounding of heart,
as that which is rent by the lips of this child?
Oh poor father! Control thyself.
Although a sudden tear must inevitably flow.
And this is caught upon his face, as by
a trembling hand, wiped dry.
He thought this weeping was of blood,
which from his heart came seeping!

He did not usually complain,
but now spoke overwhelmingly:
"What purpose, God, has your creation?
Why could you not let us remain
there within the nothingness, and where
my soul and body long to return again?
Why have you created Man,
and blessed him with a family,
when in my family's great need,
I cannot of my own blood feed them
like the pelican?.....
Be still my tongue. The Lord knows what to do.
His highly complicated plan,
the blind cannot see through.

And to question God, we are not free.
I am sent upon this sea,
and set within my soul is a compass,
there to show
in which direction of these waters,
I should go. _
Take this, my boy,
take and enjoy this little piece of bread.
It is the last, allotted for tomorrow,
but if eaten now instead,
the good Lord will know tomorrow,
how you shall be fed."

Greatly pleased,
the little boy seized it eagerly.
And on the bed rebounded
to squat there happily,
so relishing the scrap of bread,
that his eyes glowed like fireflies,
incandescently.
When swallowing the final bite,
dreaming came like twilight mist,
descending in the valley.
His drooping head sank back into the pillow,
until he slept, and dreamed the while,
his face reflecting with a smile,
the dream's delight.
I wonder what he's dreaming of,
a loaf of bread, or coffin white?

The mother softly cried herself to sleep.
Her babe is laid beside the other, while keeping

both within her firm embrace,
as she, upon the bedside edge, is sleeping.

The man rose from the table, to stealthily tread
upon tiptoe, inching his way to the bed.
And stopping before the arms interwound,
he stood there musing, without a sound:
"At last, you are happy, my loved ones!
Of life, you are now unaware.
The dream has removed from your shoulders
the weight
which is yours until sunset to bear.
My poor, dearly loved ones,
God surely, the dream loved them better than I,
when accomplishing that which I could not,
with this joy, providing them by?
But no matter, believe me,
suffice it to say, that happy are they . . .
Sleep as deeply through the night,
sleep my dearest ones. Goodnight!"

Kissing the three, and crossing them
with his hand outspread,
he made the sign of the Trinity,
above each sleeping head.
(Nothing other than this blessing,
could his hand now to them give!)
Returning to his place and casting
yet another gentle glance towards the crowded bed,
the look conveyed such sweetness,
that the sleeping ones dreamed of
keeping company with angels,

while among the roses led.
Then out into the darkness, beyond the window-pane,
he stared with such intensity,
as if from eyes aflame,
he would alight the darkened night.

PART THREE

Where can this man, so wide awake,
be travelling in the mind?
What kind of journey does he undertake?
Whom does he seek to find?
There above, and venturing amidst the heights
of a terrain, only frequented with daring
by demi-gods and the insane!

The house, and worries of the day,
were like an egg-shell cast away
as from a bird, when hatched to fly.
Within was left the body dead,
by the live inhabitant now shed.
He, of the previous family,
had now the world to hold;
The One who had embraced the three,
now millions did enfold.

On wings of mind, he flies so high,
the Earth below appears as though of paper,
smouldering and flickering with flashes,
into ashes.
In speedy flight,
as shooting past each star, they shiver
one by one, shuddering

like candlelight, when breathed upon.

Millions and millions of miles he flew,
from one sphere unto another.
And those he passed by
were suddenly left, straggling behind each other,
as trees group together within a dense wood,
when a galloping horseman rides through.

And when beyond the billionth star,
he then reached . . . from afar . . .
the end of the universe, maybe?
No . . . at the centre, now was he!
And before him stood the Ruler of the worlds,
whose every glance is of true light,
and from whose eyes, each sparkle bright,
evolves a sun.
And Earths and Moons revolve around
in orbit of each one.

Thus spake the Spirit of the man,
an ancient soul, now bathed in light,
as bathes a swan
amid translucent waters of the lake:
"Hail Lord, praise be to Thee!
One risen particle of dust has flown here unto You,
to pay You homage and to say,
Father, I remain thine own loyal son!
Hard is the course, which I am sent upon,
but I do not complain.
In fact, I bless Thee,
for You have shown your love again,
by having chosen me.

Degenerated are the Earth-dwellers,
who, having turned aside from You
are now slaves . . .
This slavery is wrought by the sins of the fathers,
and to little children brought by heredity.
Man bows down before Mankind!
Whose fellowman need bow his head,
because God is derided!
For here on Earth, you are regarded with derision
Lord.
Although this cannot be forever so.
Thy glory must be re-established.
The life Thou gavest me, my Father,
I re-dedicate to Thee.
As to the cost?
Or whether payment should be made,
I do not ask;
Even the worst slave is ready to tire,
when paid.
Yet an incentive, I require.
For without hope of acquiring
that reward which I desire,
I tire, and further tired shall be.
But greatly would I be rewarded,
if soon my people I could see
released from their enslavery.
I love them, although they are guilty.
My love transcends their sin.
For strength Lord I pray.
Lighten my way,
that I may work harder
for my fellowmen!"

Thus having spoken and descending
from the vastness of the sky,
the Spirit now returned to Earth,
where in the dim small room,
his body there benumbed,
awaited him.

A tremor shook the man,
as through his limbs there ran a cold sensation.
Yet streaming from his brow, came perspiration . . .
Had he been awake or dreaming,
was the question? . . . . .
He must have been awake, because drowsiness began.
And weighted were his eyelids by dreaminess.
The man drew his limbs together wearily.
Laboriously, he made his way
to where upon the floor, a mattress lay.

He who recently had scaled the sky,
upon the crude baled straw did lie!
While the butchers of the world,
on silken cushions took their ease,
the world's benefactor restlessly
turned about upon coarse frieze.
But look!
Mustering a final flare,
the nightlight's puny life burns out.
Yet outside, see the night dividing
and sub-dividing, like a secret
carried further by confiding.

Dawn, the gardening-maiden gay,
comes scattering roses along the way.

She throws them through the window small,
to grow against the room's cold wall.

And now,
the first ray of sunlight,
is cast upon the brow of the sleeping man.
A golden garland thus presented
with God's salutary kiss!

PART FOUR.

Oh Wonderful Being, impoverished man,
Who are you?
Your spiritual clothing is woven from starlight,
into a robe of shining hue,
yet your body is covered with rags.
Your family is hungry, and you hunger too.
And today is your Sunday, the day when for you
new bread shall appear on your table bare,
by chance apparently lying there.
And of that which you and your loved ones share,
you shall have less in proportion.
You strive for the happiness of everyone,
and although you have access to Heaven's gate,
when you knock upon the houses of the gentlemen,
they close the door before you, as you wait.
You speak with God.
And yet when you address the lordlings of the land,
they would not deign to speak with you.
By some, you are acclaimed as an apostle,
yet others have named you as a rogue.
Divine or diabolical,
Whoever may you be?

How came you into life?
What is your ancestry?
Do your parents bear your name with pride?
Or do they hide their burning faces,
upon hearing it with shame?
On what fabric were you born?
Velvet thick, or canvas worn?
Will you narrate the history of this man's life to me?

That which I shall now relate . . .
Were I to illustrate the story, it would simulate a brook.
Welling from a cliff unknown,
and tumbling down into a valley,
dark and narrowly confined,
where croaking ravens dwell.
And stumbling over every stone,
in foaming agitation
to suffer there perpetually
the pain of turbulation.

PART FIVE

The clock proclaimed the midnight hour,
one bitter winter's night,
a winter's night which brought to power
two tyrants of relentless might:
Cold and Darkness.
Under a cover, lay the world.
Who, at such an hour would try to incite God,
even below an open sky?

The streets, untrodden by the crowds,
were empty long ago,
like the dried-up river beds,

wherein no rivers flow . . .
Among the streets deserted,
but one had ventured out,
a raging, raving lunatic.
The Tempest was about.
He sped along so rapidly,
through every road and track,
it was as if the devil
were sat upon his back.
And beat his sides repeatedly
with blazing spurs of fire.
In anger, he jumped heatedly
up to the roof-tops, where
he whistled down the chimneys.
Rushing onward, he began
to cry into the deaf ears
of the blind night, as he ran.
Then with a roar, he seized the clouds
and with sharp talons, tore them into shreds.
The stars in terror trembled,
as the moon rolled helplessly
among the clouds, as if adrift
amidst a stormy sea,
like a corpse upon the waves,
borne topsy-turvily.

Within a wink, one breath he drew,
and blew the clouds again into a heap.
And from great height unto the ground,
he, swooping like a thievish bird, upon the quarry
found,
would take a window-shuttering,
to shake it hinge-free fluttering.

When those within from their deep sleep
upstarted suddenly,
he darted off into the night,
with frightful laugh of glee.

The town was deserted . . .
for who would be out in such a storm? . . .
There is however, one live form . . .
or possibly a ghost?
It has an air of ghostliness.
Coming near, now closely nigh,
it does appear to be a woman.
But darkness seals the mystery,
of whether beggar-woman, she,
or lady of society?
Most furtively, she peers around.
And seeing a carriage standing by,
treads stealthily towards it, creeping,
as the coachman steadfastly
sits upon his box there sleeping.
Without a sound,
the carriage door is opened covertly.
With intent to steal perhaps?
Nay, on the contrary.
Something brought is placed within.
The door is closed, and like a thought,
she slips away.

An entry-door soon opens for a countryman and woman.
They enter the coach.
The coachman arouses the horses.
They run . . .

A whimpering was heard inside,
then instantly, a scream . . .
The woman had cried out because
beside her feet, a baby cried.

The carriage arrives at it's destination.
The man and woman alight.
And these words to the coachman,
the woman said that night:

"Son, here is your fee.
And there in the coach is your tip.
A dear little babe.
Be sure to take good care of it,
because it is God's gift."
That was all she had to say,
the pair then went upon their way.

Poor infant, lying in the coach!
Why were you not a dog's off-spring?
Nurtured on this woman's lap,
then you would have been,
receiving nourishment administered with gentle care;
Yet because you are to grow into a man,
and not a dog,
of what shall be your destiny?
God is not unaware!

The coachmen, listening, scratched his head.
But exactly what he said,
whether it was a curse or prayer,
one could not tell.

Only that he muttered something,
for God's gift was not well-pleasing unto him.
He wondered, what should he be doing with this brat?
If taken home, the landlord there,
would soon be throwing things at him,
and then would surely cast the pair
out through the door.
Greatly aggravated, he drove the horses mercilessly,
whipping them spasmodically.

On the outskirts of the town,
a squalid tavern shows
it still holds revelry within.
How the windows from the lamplight glows,
red-shining, like a drunkard's nose.
The coachman, needing nothing more,
now placed the god-send tastefully
upon the step, against the door,
and then departed hastily.

No sooner had he gone away,
comrades within began to say goodnight.
One drunken friend, as he stepped out,
came stumbling, tumbling, just as though
he was furrowing a picture on the frozen snow.
The good man cursed that such as he,
upright and of dignity,
should fare so badly,
protesting madly,
"That step, has grown since yesterday.
Yesterday, 'twas not so high,
for if it had been, then would I
have also stumbled yesterday.

But I did not stumble yesterday,
yet did not drink less than today,
because unto the minute do
I drink what I drink every day."

Thus grumbling,
he struggled to his feet again,
and staggered off, continuously mumbling:
"I spoke in vain.
The step, though greater, is the same,
the same as it was yesterday!
Already here, now I recall,
my standing clear had been unsteady.
How I did rear upon my legs!
And yet no matter where I veered,
still had I left in shame.
Yes. Obviously that step has grown ...
'Less someone there had placed a stone?
That could very well be so, for oh,
the world is bad.
Malevolent delight is had, by causing stumbling.
'Tis folk are bad. This I repeat.
Folk are of ill intent.
They trundle stones low 'neath my legs,
and for the blindness of my feet,
my nose has to repent.
The only comfort I receive,
is that when the others leave,
they shall trip head over heels also.
I would dearly love to be
in hiding, stopping there to see
them one by one a-dropping as they go!
He-he-he.

But what are you saying old man? Is this right?
Does such malicious delight befit you?
No. To my own self, I am not true.
And so for this, I shall atone
by returning to the the door, from where,
I'll cast away the stone.
A thief am I, and sometimes led
to even strike a robbers head,
if it is his due.
But that a nose should be so battered
as was mine before,
to have that upon my conscience,
I could not endure."

Slowly the stout-hearted fellow returned,
to fling the offending stone afar.
And later, reaching for it .... shaking,
oh what screams were in the making!
The old man was so flabbergasted,
"Thundering thunderbolts," he blasted.
And to himself, he said:
"Never have I held before, a stone so soft,
or furthermore, a stone that yelled!
I must admit,
a screaming stone, sounds odd a bit.
Let me see it clearly by the window near ...
Gently now, I do believe it is a child.
This truly is a child.
Good evening, little brother dear,
or sister, should I say ...
What you are, I do not know.
How the devil came you here?

Are you used to being from your parents, in this way?
You unruly little so-and-so!
But what am I saying, yet again,
such speech as this, is quite insane!
Why, the poor little thing
is still bound up in swaddling,
perhaps but newly-born today.
Who are the parents?
If I could return it to them,
then I would without delay.
This nevertheless is such wickedness
to cast the child away, as if it were a worn out shoe.
Pigs, nor even robbers, this, they wouldn't do.
It's wrapped within an old torn dress.
'Tis a poor woman's child ...
Hm, but supposin' 'twas born in wealthiness?
And for that reason and no other,
clothed in these rags, to conceal the mother,
the ancestry, that none should guess?
Who can tell?
There is not anyone to know.
This already is a mystery,
and shall remain forever so.
Who is to be a father, poor little child to thee?
Who is to be your father?
Why, I myself shall be!
Upon my word of honour,
thy father, I will be.
And why not?
I would rear you in respectability.
For naturally, I'll steal for you,
as long as I have the ability.
And when I am too old to work,

you then could steal for me.
Thus one hand washes the other.
Oh, it will be fine.
Now thefts of mine should be more lawful than before,
as I will be stealing for both of us,
and even less, my conscience gnaw.
But what a commotion!
I must get some milk for you.
This for sure is true. Milk . . .
Whoa, not to worry. Why,
there is a neighbour close nearby,
whose babe was buried yesterday.
She soon will take care of the suckling,
and on that you can rely.
Make no mistake that for good payment,
even the devil himself would try."

Trudging homewards thoughtfully,
the old fellow went,
through narrow alleys leading to
a dwelling hidden underground,
with but a cellar vent.
From her sleep, the neighbour was awakened by the sound
of a fist a-hammering,
and the screeching of the door,
at being struck, a-clamouring.

"Neighbour, light the candle.
Quickly", said the man.
"Either get the candle, or
I shall set the house afire.
What for? What for? Why bother question me?

The candle when I say. Immediately!
So . . . now that is done, you may proceed to feed this
child.
Where did I get it? I found it indeed.
This is God's blessing for me to receive.
I have always been professing to be loved by God.
And truly, He must love me more
than do the priests believe.
Hm. Such great treasure!
And this I now entrust to thee, Neighbour.
Take even better care of him, than were he thine own son.
Raise him, and regarding the expenses of his rearing,
I myself shall settle every one.
Let us come to an agreement.
Why, we can surely reach an understanding,
you and I.
It is true that nowadays
the money comes in short supplies.
And that's because, the devil knows,
all people have a hundred eyes;
Yet none the less, but regally,
with God's help, so shall I pay thee.
But take good care of him always,
because to me, this child you see,
is like my very eyesight.
He is the hope of my old days."

Arrangements were made,
The half-frozen baby warmed through as he laid
at the breast.
Of this, his mouth had taken hold,
and bitter life was sweetly drawn.
Though yet only one day old,

what buffeting already borne!
What buffeting as yet untold!

PART SIX.

Early next morning,
the old man had called upon his neighbour
to inquire:
"How is the guest? I hope that he is well.
But in here, there is a chill.
You hag of a neighbour, stoke the fire . . .
Have I not stressed one hundred times
that I shall pay the bill? . . .
Though whether for a boy or girl?
Still I do not know."

"A boy, my friend. 'Tis a boy alright.
His lordship is as sharp and bright as a bird."

"So much the better.
In seven or eight years, he'll make such a thief.
Christlike, he'll be;
This illustrious thief shall be trained by me!
For truth to tell, at this I excel,
and could thus train the child, like none other.
I also taught blind Thomas, who they hanged a while ago . . .
There was a thief for you!
Though but one-eyed, he stealthiwise
had stolen the God of a thousand eyes. –
My son, do not fear. Upon my oath here,
I promise that neither shall bungling arise
from thy labour.
But Neighbour,

the name perhaps we should supply,
which unto the world, he would be known by.
What think you my angel, what could we call him? . . .
Well, let me see.
What day was yesterday? . . .
'Twas New Year's Eve. Silvester's Day . . . .
Right. Silvester, so be it.
We'll have a christening ceremony.
I will be priest, and you, the Godmother.
At least, to give the name legality.
And in accord with Christianity,
not albeit the profanity of heathen times,
as ere instruction given to our holy brother Peter,
from the very gate of Heaven.
Is water in this pot? . . . There is a drop, I see.
Lift up the child and bring him unto me . . .
But stop. If indeed the priest am I,
then I must have a cassock.
Where is a sack which I can tie around my neck?"

The sack was found,
and round the old man, neatly bound.
Dipping his hand in the water, he,
with all due pomp,
ceremoniously christened the boy.
And Silvester became his name.

PART SEVEN.

Four years passed by.
The babe became a youngster small.
He grew up in the darkness, underneath the ground.

The single dwelling, he did share with sin and vermin.
He never breathed the sky's pure air,
nor was he ever led to see Earth's beauty,
for he lived there like the dead.

The old man took delight therein,
for sense and reason flashed from him
as sparks are struck from flint-stone.
And thinking came;
as from a spark, arose a flame.

Barely four years old, the child
already stole successfully,
from the apple-woman.
And from the hat of the blind beggarman,
he also stole the penny.
For his caution,
his good tutor gave him kindly words and bread,
but at the same time clouted him,
when the day had passed away,
without him having stolen any.
This however, rarely happened.

The old man's hopes grew visibly.
No effort did he spare,
as on a futuristic rock,
he built his castles in the air.
Until one day, he stuck suspended,
indefatigably there!
The painstaking poor old fellow
on the gallows, he did swing.
He, who was deserving so much more.

Witnessing the hanging, was his neighbour.
She had seen the master with the noose around his neck.
And his tongue, thrust out at length, as though
with some derision at the world,
for having put him there like that,
to be derided so.
After the performance, the woman homeward sped,
and this, unto the little boy, then she sweetly said:

"Now you can go to the devil, my son.
God speed you into hell!
As from today, I get no pay,
And here at my expense,
to be well fattened like the goose,
you could not wish to stay.
Come. This kindness will I do for you,
by showing you the door.
But if you dare return, I shall
be throwing all of thee in the canal."

Bewildered, the little boy dumbly obeyed.
When the door behind him shut,
but one glance, he darted back,
startled by the noise it made.
Then slowly, he departed.

Away he went a-wandering,
out of the one street and into the other.
So long a street, he had never known,
nor ever seen so many fine and fancy shops,
or among such strangers been.
All was so new to him, that he stood
gazing open-mouthedly . . .

then slowly ventured further.
As he left one street,
there was always another,
to endlessly be walked on down,
without ever reaching the end of the town.

So much walking, and such wonder,
had fatigued the little boy.
And now he was exhausted from it all.
Stooping, sinking, settling,
at the corner of the street,
he huddled, with his head against the wall.
Across the way,
two lively children were at play,
making merry with a coloured toy.
He stared at them and smiled as though
there, he played with them also.
Until at last they stared at him,
as slowly, he was falling fast asleep.

Long he slept;
Until within a nightmare,
he dreamed of an advancing pair
of red hot irons,
each with a searing spike.
They kept on coming nearer,
nearing his eyes, as if intending
these to strike . . .
In dread of the ordeal impending,
he screamed, for want of courage ending sleep,
to awaken terror-shaken.

Now it is the late of night.

In the sky, the stars are out,
in the street, no folk about,
except for one old crone.
She stands before him, there alone,
with staring eyes,
of which he's even more in fear
than of the irons within his dream.
She draws near.

She came so close to where he sat,
that soon his head was pressing flat
against the corner-stone,
not daring for to look upon
the withered witch-like old woman,
nor daring yet to look away.
She gently stroked his brow and cheek,
endeavouring to sweetly speak,
as kindly, she did say:
"What is your name, my little son?
Who is your father? Who is your mother?
Where do you live?
Come now, I'll soon take you home.
Give unto me your hand."

"Silvester is my name . . .
I haven't a father, or mother, nor ever had,
for I was found.
And I mustn't go home any more;
Neighbour there has promised me:
that if I dare return, then she
is going to throw me in the canal,
where I'll be drowned."

"Well, come with me, my little one.
Come to me. Thy mother, I will be.
Your kindly mother, who will take good care of you.
So . . . let us go."

Catching hold of the old woman's hand,
the child followed her timorously,
with an almost vacant air,
tremulously not knowing
what would become of him, or where
he was going?

"Look, we live here, my little son,"
said the old woman when finally home.
"This room is mine,
and that to be thine, is the kitchen.
But you will not be alone . . .
Hey Doggie, Doggie . . . . Sit!
Here it is . . . Isn't he a nice little puppy-dog?
Settle down with him, my dear.
There is room for both of you on this rug.
With such a good bed,
you could not be wanting a better one.
And the puppy shall now keep you warm.
Don't be afraid. He's a good little dog.
He won't harm you.
See how lovingly he looks upon you,
and how much he wags his tail?
Doubtless, you shall love one another,
as each would love his brother.
Lie down beside him and sleep, my son.
Perhaps you are hungry?

I would give you supper,
but as it is so late,
I can see you sleeping badly,
if that, now you ate.
And as for little children,
or so it seems to me,
to sup before they go to sleep,
is bad especially.
For thereby comes a-dreaming with the devil.
So now lie down, and go to sleep, my lad."

The old woman left him there and then;
Trailing apprehensively
around the dog, about the rug,
he drew himself eventually unto the outer edge.
Near to his companion,
he did not dare to stay.
But irrepressibly,
the puppy snuggled up to where he lay.
His bright eyes were a-glistening
with such a kindly light,
and shone with such affection
through the darkness of the night,
that trust and courage
were engendered in the little boy.
To each other, they drew nigh,
closer, until now close by
the child began to stroke the puppy's fur.
And as he smoothed it into place,
he was licked upon the face, in co-ordination.
Then at last, the little boy broke into conversation.
And as he spoke, the animal,

listening, gave a cry,
softly whining, whimpering,
by way of his reply.
And the two became true friends.

But the very next day,
the old harridan had this to say:
"Now listen to me, my son.
As you can imagine,
I'll not support you for nothin'.
Not even Christ's coffin
was guarded for nothin'.
You'll have work to do.
Because as it is written: He
who doesn't work, shall neither eat.
Nevertheless, the work shall be
as light as a lord's comparatively . . .
You'll have to beg.
There's nothin' else that you can do.
And I am loth to do this work
because I've grown too fat.
It wards off the people.
So merciless, are they,
that when I beg, it only serves
to drive them all away.
Well, dear son, in my place now,
you must beg instead.
They will be compassionate,
and when they bring unto you gifts,
tell them that you are an orphan,
and your father's dead.
Your mother's lying ill at home,
dying of starvation.

I'll be waiting at a distance,
watching what you do.
So for that very reason,
you had better watch out too.
Otherwise, this I can stake upon my reputation,
your days shall not be happy ones,
but full of tribulation.
If you are good,
then so shall I be very good,
'though very bad I'll be, if you are bad.
Have this written in your head,
and on your heart, dear lad.
You are to beg from everyone
whose clothes are better than thine own.
You'll find that is sufficient, do not fear.
Stand before them meekly,
with your head upon one side,
and be reaching out your hand.
Appear
in tears,
by moistening your eyes,
and puckering your eyebrows in a frown.
And purse
your lips,
to put
your mouth
a-pouting, a-tremulously down.
And thus you'll cry, beseeching the people ere they go,
in the name of thy sick mother,
and God's Holy Name also.
Do you understand this now my child?
If not, I'll explain it yet again.

But after all my words repeating,
if you haven't learnt this teaching,
I'll be then a-beating it into you with a cane."

She placed the child to enact the part,
in order to learn it all by heart,
and not forget it.
And when they both rehearsed the scene,
the boy was then dismayed,
on learning of the trickery, used within the trade.

"A gold mine, I have found in thee,
dear little son. He-he-he!"
cackled the old crone.
We shall truly live like lords,
like lords, we'll truly be!
Let us go unto the harvest, immediately.
You are hungry?
When of payment in receipt,
you soon may have enough to eat.
But you mustn't eat a lot, not you especially,
lest you could be getting fat like me.
The stick would then be striking
at the imprint of the hare
that got away.
The fat beggar must, you know,
for alms, within a thin one go."

They sought a street more crowded.
There, the woman stood the child,
then into a tavern, she crept nearby,
from where she kept a-peeping out,

the reaping to espy.
And as many times as there was dropping
something into the boy's hand,
she took up a glass of brandy,
chuckling, gulping each one down,
a-tippling without stopping.

PART EIGHT

Each day continued as before,
the poor boy begged, yet starved the more;
The woman's only care was that
he should not put on any fat.
Nought else from life he ever drew,
he begged, he starved. 'Twas all he knew.

Many times, he had watched the children at their play,
and staring at a group had thought,
wouldn't that game have been good,
if only that he also could
have played with them that way!

As from day to day, his intelligence matured,
he became aware of his intense unhappiness.
He now had lived in beggary, for no less than two years.
No more was there need to moisten his eyes,
for these were so frequently filled with tears.

The child had but a single friend,
who looked upon him lovingly,
loving him, as he was loved.
And eagerly he shared with him the meagre scraps of food,
which he received at home,

and those of which he found around the town . . .
This one true friend, the puppy bright,
his close companion of the night.

Every morning, he was grieving,
yearning for the dog, as leaving.
When returning, oh what joy,
in late evening, for the boy!

The old woman was eaten with jealousy.
Resentful of the friendship formed,
and that the dog now loved the child
much more than it did she.
'Twas beaten many times, and when
the animal in pain, howled bitterly,
the child had sobbed his heart out.
At last, the woman drove it from the house.
But though, 'twas beat on every limb,
it still came running back to him,
to love the little boy the more
than ever was he loved before.

Thus the child existed.
Now six years old, he had endured
six centuries of wretchedness,
experiencing but a few
moments of true happiness.

One late autumn evening,
at the corner of the street,
there, he stood a-shuddering from the cold.
Mud lay on the roadway, densely overspread

by dismal fog, oppressively descending overhead.
Bare-headed, with bare feet he stood,
amid the mist and mud.
To those passing by, he cried,
extending a tiny yellow hand.
His cry, unto the heart, kept striking
like an agonizing pain.
And rang out with the plaintive sounding
of a church bell, when resounding
for a man about to die.

A fiercesome old man came and stood by his side,
to give him close scrutinization.
So long was he there,
and so piercing his stare,
in appraisal of the situation,
that the child then made ready to run.
"Stop!" the old gentleman crossly cried.
The child, in obeyance stood fast,
not daring yet to move, until
the gentleman queried at last:
"Haven't you parents?"

"I . . ." he began, intending to say,
I have a sick mother a-starving of hunger,
my father is dead.
The words stuck in his throat.
He thought how the man should have known this by now.
And to such a severe man, he dared not to lie,
so he said:

"I haven't any parents, though
whether they exist or not,

that I wouldn't know.
A foundling am I."

"Then follow me," was the reply.

But no sooner had the boy begun,
than the lurking old woman rushed out,
leaving her place of hiding, to shout:
"You remain here, you lying brat! . . .
Master, that boy is my son!"

"Sir," the child entreated, "Sir,
I am not her son.
Save me, in the name of God and Holy Saints!
Take me with you.
I am tired of beggary;
She always makes me beg for her,
while I am made to starve.
And only so that I'll appear to be of sickly pallor,
so that who-so looks at me,
the more compassionate should be.
Oh my God, how I am starving even now!"

Thus the child had spoken,
looking upward at the dour gentleman.
And from imploring eyes,
there downward ran a tear,
and then the tears began a-pouring in a shower.

"Oh you godless wicked devil,
born of devil's seed!"
bellowed the old woman at the boy.

"You're not fit to be used as a sole of a shoe,
You're a headful of lies, and bad all through,
without a bit of of good in you!
But that my son should beg for me.
Master, I am shamed to death
whenever he goes begging.
'Tis his bad habit to do this, as soon as I avert my eyes.
Yet how many times have I beaten him now,
in trying to make him realise
how much shame
is brought unto my name!
I am poor, but have no need of begging,
for I live by honest labour.
And yet that I,
should make him beg!
I!
Only the best crumbs drop from my mouth.
And I eat my fill!
But never mind all this . . .
yet you deny me still.
You odious fiend, you loathsome brat.
Is there not pain within your heart,
that you deny your mother,
your own mother, yet again!
Are you not torn apart?
How can these words issue from you,
and not come with your stomach too,
your lungs and spleen and liver?
There is not on Earth,
a better grandmother than I,
nor could there be
as bad a grandson, there as he!

But his judgement is already nigh . . .
The ownership of her child, soon,
his mother will deny."

The woman kept rattling on like an old mill,
re-iterating on one breath until;
Here, the stern gentleman managed to say:
"Enough of this nonsense,
or I, with this stick, will put you to silence!
Despicable hag!
You're as drunk as a tap;
When you are sober, then bring to me,
his baptism certificate for me to see.
(The large house there, is where I live.)
And you can take the child away.
But on condition that you come with the certificate.
Now be off with you . . . and as for thee,
boy, follow me."

The boy, following the man,
looked back frequently,
imagining that he was followed
by the old woman, and that she
was reaching out, and just about
to seize his collar;
But to advance, she did not dare.
There she remained on the spot.
She could only threaten with her fists,
and roll her eyes, with growing ire,
glaring, like the red hot irons,
glowing from the smithy's fire.

PART NINE

Work was lighter for the boy.
No more was he made to steal,
Nor was he made to beg.
What sweet charity, oh what joy!
But there were times when the hawk of anxiety
swooped down upon him, breathtakingly:
What if the woman came with a certificate,
what would become of him then? . . .
And there were times when upon him would softly descend
the dove of deep sorrow,
as into his mind came the loyal little dog,
his sleeping companion and friend.
And then for his sake, he could hardly refrain
from rushing back to the old woman again,
and even returning to beggary, so
that he and the dog could together remain.

He dreamed of seeing him, holding him close,
and felt the dog licking his hand.
But when he awakened without his dear friend,
and realised that he was gone,
he started to cry, and for long afterwards,
his sorrowing lingered on.

When first he arrived at the gentleman's house,
the boy was entrusted to servants.
He was then scrubbed clean of the filth and grime,
encrusted upon him for so long a time.
He received in place of his worn out rags,
some fine new clothes.
How pleased he was!

He believed that until now, he had not lived,
and was but newly-born.
By then had the gentleman sent for him,
and with severity said,

"Boy, the child you see here, is my son.
He is the young master, whom you must revere,
and call Sir.
He will give you orders, and you'll accept his word,
for he will be Lord over thee.
His servant, you will be.
Or, like his word, so shall your work
be unacceptable to me.
Within a wink, you must do
precisely what he orders you;
If you fulfill your obligations,
then no trouble should arise.
You shall eat and you shall drink,
and will be clothed . . . otherwise
the ragged tatters which you wore
when first you were employed,
shall be strung around your neck.
And so, into the world you'll go
to beg, as you have begged before."

The orphan served attentively his esteemed young master.
He became his shadow, which ever round him played.
He walked behind him, stood behind him
fleetingly espying
his master's lips, for any movement made.
And hardly was spoken to him a command,
than it was obeyed.

Yet how much more, the good boy would endure!

The young master was a scoundrel,
as young masters, generally.
The boy was made to feel that he was lord.
Mentally and physically,
made to feel, literally,
all of the indignities of being at his heel.

When his mouth was scalded by the soup,
on the little servant's cheek,
it then was spat;
When others had not greeted him,
deferentially,
then was battered from the little head,
the hat.
When the comb had tugged his hair,
as it lay entangled there,
then was pulled the youngster's hair, so viciously.
Such wickedness was perpetrated,
soon as it was contemplated.
He deliberately would tread upon his feet,
and then give the boy a push,
for why be standing in the street?
Mud was smeared upon him,
then for being so unclean,
the dastard boxed his ears,
and poured water over him.
And if the boy burst into tears,
he was called a puny bastard.
So much the poor boy suffered,
yet he daily suffered more,
but patiently his troubles bore.

All was bravely tolerated,
as dealt from someone manly,
in whom high spirits dwelt.

And what could be gained by such toleration?
Why did he not run from that place of torment,
as so often had been his intention?
If you but knew why he remained!

It was not good food and clothing,
which lured him to return,
when he ventured on the road to hide
within the great world wide;
He was not like the goose or hen,
to roam around while loose, and then
in hungering, bound to return unto the place
where substantial food was found.
Yet if the door were opened for
the imprisoned lark or nightingale,
it would fly away for ever.
They would readily leave good food behind
for whatever they could in freedom find.
The boy felt like the bird,
yet he, although desiring to be free,
did like the goose and hen remain.
And when he strayed,
came back again!
What decoy had lured the boy into returning?
Learning.

He learned with his young master,
as behind him, there he stood.

Peeping unnoticed into his book,
while taking note with every look
and paying attention
to that which the tutor was saying.
And what he once learnt,
he remembered outright.
Long before the master,
he knew how to read and write.

His knowledge grew with every year,
increasing like the branching
of antlers on the deer.
And he took pride within himself,
whenever he could hear
the master speaking stupidly,
as he so often did.
He inwardly corrected him, yet for a while
unable to restrain a smile
at his absurdities.

The servant's superiority o'er the master,
in the presence of the tutor,
had not passed unnoticed.
Or the blush shown by the pupil,
when he had not known the lesson,
and the servant had then told him what to say.
For after that was heard,
he could relate it word for word.
This was to the credit of the boy,
yet it was not to accredit any joy.
No. Because the haughty young master was humiliated so,
every time that he was put to shame.

And every day,
new and harsher harassments were made upon the boy,
who daily suffered more,
from the indignities he bore.
Now when the master struck him,
he felt not the flesh a-smarting
and a-reddening aflame,
but his spirit, in the blushing
realisation of his shame.

He was sixteen.
Day by day, an additional ray of light came gleaming,
streaming through the mists within his mind.
And every shaft of insight clear,
had formed a letter, until composed of many letters,
was the inscription:

"By what right, am I beaten here?
For what good reason does man trouble man?
Has God created one man better than another?
The Lord preached righteousness,
but that which is righteous is not done.
Yet without discrimination, He loves all men equally.
And I will not endure any more,
no matter what happens to me.
Food and clothing I received, and accommodation,
but my situation as their servant has repaid the debt.
It is just, that I must work,
but not to take the beatings.
Yet only once may he strike me, then by my God, I swear,
more than that, I shall not bear!"

And so it came to pass,

that on the following occasion
when the master raised his hand,
(and he did not have to wait so very long,)
he then raised his voice to cry:
"Stop!
You shall not wrong me any more,
for I shall so retaliate,
that you will rue it 'til the day you die!
I have been a dog for long enough.
One whom you could beat and kick beneath your feet.
But I have since become a man, for though a servant I may be,
created also Man, was he!
I admit that one hand here, has laid upon me benefit.
But by the other was I beaten with a stick.
Therefore there is nothing that can hold us to each other."
The young master was astounded at this surprising speech.
He was stricken paralytic by the shock.
And frothing at the mouth, his voice rising in a screech,
spluttered: "Scurrilous rebel, born of servant stock!"

Instantly the boy replied,
his voice, disparaging in tone:
"Hm, servant-born?
Considering that the birth's unknown,
my father, a nobleman could be,
of a finer lineage than thine own.
And if that he had disowned me,
'twas his misdeed, not mine.
If gentlemen are such as thee,
and all so wicked hearted,
then it is as well for me,

that from him was I parted.
And for this would I thank him too,
as I prefer to be a man of noble honour true.
And a rebel . . . .
If it is rebellious for man to feel that he is man,
the same as any other,
and that this he should proclaim,
then proudly do I say:
I am a rebel.
Yet were I to declare
all that of which I am aware,
it would incite millions with me to unite in rebellion.
And all the world would tremble,
like the trembling of Spartacus,
when he, the wall did see,
cleft by the gladiators, with the chains of their captivity!
God be with you, illustrious master.
Together, we cannot remain.
For I have spoken to you as a man.
And once that a servant has uprisen thus,
though he die of hunger, or high on the gallows-tree,
no longer can he, a servant be!"

He turned about, and went from there, without a backward
look.
And left the house forever, where
his childhood had drifted away like a flower
within a muddy brook.

Aimlessly into the world, he strode,
along any direction going.
The ardour of Youth had enkindled his heart,
now glowing, like the fire ablaze within the sky,

at which, the whistling wind-storm giant was blowing;
What fascinating pictures of legendary myths,
were seen originating in these flames!
The effect upon his soul, of this conflagration,
was like the tempering of steel, at the smiths.

At the end of the town, he was there overtaken
by the young master's tutor
who, in trying to reach him, was so running-shaken
that the good fellow could hardly find breath for his speech.
Gasping, and stopping,
his face, he kept mopping,
as sweat poured persistently,
while in the meantime, he spoke
incoherently:

"Take this money. Do, my son.
One year's wages, have I here,
which should support you for one year,
if used with discretion.
I tell you now, that you could be
a man of great distinction.
I have never known a boy, more praise-worthy than thee.
Word for word, what you spoke out,
was that which I had felt about,
but never dared to say.
And when I heard your conversation,
I stood in awe with admiration.
May God bless you for those words.
I advise, nay command, yea command you boy,
to continue with your studies and complete your education,
or my curse upon thee shall be God's defeat.

You were not born for thine own self,
but for thy nation and the world.
So I repeat that you must study,
though after all is said and done,
this really goes without the saying,
for you dearly love to learn.
God bless you now, my son.
Be lucky.
Live to prosper.
I ask of thee, remember me from time to time, and yet,
if you take not my advice,
then me, you can forget."

The boy now fell upon his knees
to kiss the good man's hand,
but this, he would not allow.
Indeed it was the lad himself,
embraced and kissed upon the brow.
And there were tears within the tutor's eyes,
before he turned to go.
How this shower of affection
was to please the poor boy so!
It was his first experience of love.
Yet sixteen years was he obliged to live
and bear affliction,
ere such a man was met,
one at last, who would not shun
the arms of the Embracing One!

PART TEN
The youth had sought to leave the town.
Emerging through it's narrow walls, he thought:
Release from prison.

And he caught his breath hungrily,
savouring there, the clean air,
God's priceless gift that brings
strength and sinew to the leg,
while adding to the spirit, wings.

Once, much later, he glanced back.
The youth had advanced far from the town.
Houses were huddled and merging together.
Bronze spires were half swallowed up by the mist.
And thousands of sounds, surging from there
were drumming in resonant tone,
like the drone of bees humming.
"Further, still further,"
he found himself urging:
"where nothing is heard, nor anything seen
of this place, where I have been living 'til now:
could the life that was mine, be called living somehow."
And he ran without slacking,
as if by a whip cracking.

Only when the town had disappeared from sight,
and he stood within boundlessness,
did he feel quite free.
"I'm free!" he called out suddenly,
"I'm free!"
He was unable to say any more,
but his tears had spoken for him
and were telling of his feelings,
far better than could speech.
Oh, what notions and emotions gather instantaneously,
when a man is first aware that he is free!

The youth then travelled on and on.
In whichever direction lay beauty's allurement,
his steps were directed that way.
He marvelled at the mountain, and also at the plain,
to see the tiers of forest peaks,
and meadow-land low-lain.
With all which now appeared in sight,
he was enthralled,
because everything before him was so new.
It was the first he saw of Nature,
and the loveliness she bore.

Crags amassed in countless numbers,
to rear among the clouds.
And the river, rumbling, thundering past,
with a clamouring as loud, as the last day of judgement . . . .
In the wide countryside of the plains,
where dumbly there dawdles the untroubled brook,
the greatest of sounds, is the buzzing of insects . . .
Here, stood the youth, with enraptured look.

When sight and spirit had taken in
the magnificence of the horizon,
he grew strongly aware of a Holy presence,
and he knelt, in prayer:

"I worship Thee, God;
And now that I know,
who are You?
Many times have I spoken thy name,
and have often heard it,
but had never felt it's touch.

Great Nature has explained to me,
Your goodness and authority . . .
Glory, Glory be to Thee, forever!
I worship Thee, God;
And now that I know,
who are You?"

Wherever he wandered, everywhere,
such beauty was seen of Nature there,
and yet he saw that everywhere,
Man was so unhappy;
Villainy and poverty were causing so much misery.
And he began to notice that
he was not the most unfortunate.
It greatly troubled him to see
that there were hundreds such as he.
In the face of their distress,
his own misfortune grew the less,
until it was forgotten totally.
And he could feel no sorrow other
than the sorrows of the others.
Upon a cold stone, he laid his head,
and burning, bitter tears were shed.

PART ELEVEN

The youth kept in mind, his promise made earnestly,
when the kind tutor had gave him the money,
ere taking his leave;
He bore this in mind, for he would not allow
mere idle words to become of his vow.
He entered a school, and studied there diligently,
where among his companions,

he shone like the moon amid stars.
They regarded him with wonder,
yet withholding their affection.
His intellectual superiority weighed upon them like a rock.
In opposition had arisen Mockery and Jealousy,
continually darting stinging barbs.
And often unto them, said he,
placidly, goodheartedly,
"Why do you trouble me, my friends?
Why do you trouble me?
'Tis not for my own benefit, that I must study so,
it is for thee.
Of what knowledge, I acquire,
trust, believe that my desire is
for others to gain by it,
and not me.
Could you but see into my soul,
and through your frailties.
And not keep hacking at the branches of the tree,
which should in time, provide for thee, thy fruit and shade.
Poor, short-sighted men, are ye!
Yet even still,
you shall love me. Yes, by my God, you will!"

After such speech, came an upstart of laughter.
It served only to provide them
with new weapons to deride him,
which struck unto the heart.

And from the world fast running wild,
he gradually withdrew into himself
eventually avoiding everyone . . . .

His friend was the unperturbed Solitude,
with whom, he was never disturbed.

He lived among illusory images,
whose wraith-like phantoms clung unto the world,
and yet he knew
that truly, they were living beings,
for in the spirit, he looked upon their future forms.

There, in seclusion, the young man would zealously,
as do believers who read the Koran,
and as too, the Bible is read by the Jews,
he there, as assiduously read of world history.
History of the World! An astonishing book!
All others had read from his look.

To one, comes salvation, the other damnation.
One has life, and the other has death.
To one, there is given a sword in the hand,
as to him is spoken this command:
"Go and fight!
You'll not be fighting uselessly, but to help humanity."
To another it is said:
"Lay down thy sword, you fight in vain.
The plight of the world shall ever remain,
as it has been and forever will be,
throughout millenniums, ceaselessly."

What read the youth from this?
What thoughts were assembling
as closed was his book, by a trembling hand? . . . .
He reflected:

"The grape is a tiny fruit, and yet
has the need of all summer, to ripen it.
The Earth too, is a fruit, a gigantic fruit.
If the grape should have need of one summer,
then how many summers are needed to bring
this so great a fruit unto ripening?
It may yet take thousands or millions of years,
but will surely at some time mature.
And when this occurs, then sumptuously
shall people eat of it, until the world's end.
The grape is ripened by sunbeams;
How many sunbeams must breathe there upon it
the warmth, ere that one became sweet?
How many thousands, how many millions of sunbeams? . . .
The Earth is also ripened by rays,
though these are not shed by the sun.
Here, they are created by soul-light.
All the Great Spirits reflect a bright stream,
but from only the great, can one originate,
so these very seldom appear:
How can I therefore, expect Earth be mature? . . . .
I feel that I too, am a ray,
and so am enabling to bring
the Earth unto its ripening.
The sunray lives but for a day,
and I know by the time of the great harvesting,
that I shall have set long ago.
My trivial work shall be lost without trace,
among the tremendous work then taking place.
But that my life was of power, would convey
satisfaction, by knowing at the hour of my death,
that I too, even I, was a ray! –

Well now, my soul, arise to work!
Let not a day nor minute stray.
Great is the aspiration.
Time flies, yet life itself
is of a brief duration. –
What is sought by the world?
Happiness!
By what means or manner?
Freedom! Yes.
I must fight for freedom,
as so many fought of yore,
even though I too must fail,
as have so many failed before!
I solemnly vow,
ye heroes of liberty,
I, among thy ranks,
now unto thy banner,
do pledge loyalty.
And should within my blood there be
one revolutionary drop,
I will gouge it from me,
though it were to start
within the centre of my heart!"

Thus was the declaration made . . .
unheard by man, yet heard of God.
And taking up the self-same book,
wherein the martyrs are recorded,
was written now therein,
Silvester's name.

PART TWELVE

The child became a youth,

the youth became a man.
Year after year came to visit the land,
departing without a farewell.
Yet they were not to pass him by.
Each one confronting him, had left its trace,
indelibly marking both heart and face.

His schooling was now over.
This had finished long ago.
And he lived among the people,
where man is so jostled at every step taken,
that part of the lustre is rubbed from his spirit,
as erased from his cheek, is the glow.

He saw how this world
was other than that
which he had supposed it to be!
Daily, less pleasing unto him was Man,
who sank into deeper degeneracy.
Man, created by God,
and in His own likeness, has eyes
to scrutinize the sun,
yet peers instead within the dust,
as if to seek from creeping things, instruction
how to crawl.
And the less to his liking, mankind proved to be,
the greater he saw was that work,
unto which he felt the call.

But he was not discouraged.
All was perhaps, of slight avail,
as when he used his voice,
yet he was equally as tireless.

Within restricted radius,
his spirit diffused light.

Having earned a reputation, as a scholar of morality,
when finishing his education,
several men had offered him
fine and lucrative appointments,
using such enticements as:

"Come and work for me,
'tis true, a servant you will be,
but to serve a master such as I,
is to thy honour. That is why
you are to bow to me.
Yet shall a thousand bow to thee.
You'll not be labouring like these,
they can be sweated as much as you please,
according to thy ability.
This is light and easy work, from which
you will grow rich."

Silvester thanked them courteously,
but of this easy work, said he:
"On account of the servants that I would acquire,
thy servant, I could not be.
I do not desire of my fellowmen
that they should kow-tow before me.
And yet you require nothing other than this,
that I should bow down before thee;
I do not regard anyone as the least,
nor would I deem anyone greater.
And as for wealth, though it were free,

such riches perhaps, were not for me,
let alone at the tremendous cost
of others being fleeced!"
Thus was his usual reply,
with cap in hand,
but head raised high.

High positions were rejected.
But when the poor invited him to be their parish scribe,
the youth had willingly and joyfully accepted.
And as the locals flocked around him when arriving
at the village,
with glowing eyes he said:
"To you people, Salutations!
Look into my eyes. See,
thy father and teacher, I will be.
What is since birth, hammered into your head?
Your duties and obligations;
But I'll teach thee, your rights!"

Silvester kept his promise. And after this,
the farmers, after finishing their work,
had not gone into the taverns, as they had always done.
Before the parish hall they stood, within a semi-circle.
And they listened with the old,
to what the youthful scribe was saying,
yet paying more attention than when listening to the priests,
because he spoke more eloquently.
And what they learned was taken home,
and to their sons retold.
The scribe was treated reverently.

But in the village, were two houses

where instead of blessings, curses
were heaped upon the young apostle's head.
These two houses were those wherein
the priest and lord of the parish dwelt,
the manor and presbytery.
They daily housed more hate and fear
of the scribe and his instruction,
for if he stayed, they both could see
themselves diminishing totally,
and so planned his destruction.

But living at the manor, was another person who
was revered by Silvester, such as he was by the people.
One pleased to hear his praises sung,
and yet alternately distressed,
on hearing slander too.
Who was this individual?
Who, in so bad a light,
could recognise a priceless picture,
and assess its worth aright?
Who? The young lady of the manor,
who would have incidentally,
preferred another destiny! . . . . .

This lady's heart was a heavenly place.
Her door was shut to Selfishness,
who gained admittance but by stealth,
or by means of force.
Yet ajar this door had stood,
to all of beauty and of good.
Truth, though hounded everywhere,
had always found a refuge there.

Heavenly, heavenly was the heart
of this lady fair!

The youth did not even guess
he had a friend and patroness,
living at the dwelling of the aristocrat.
And such a lovely patroness!
He saw the dear girl now and then
as when she walked unto the village,
or from her window, gazed outside,
at the surrounding countryside.
After seeing her, then he
would spend much time in reverie.
An inexplicably wonderful feeling
overcame him, softly stealing through his heart,
which unto him, did this impart:

"A man's not just a citizen,
he also is a man.
Should one forever live for others, and never for oneself?
You poor man, by the time that you can live for your own self,
shall you, yourself have any time to live?
You divide your heart among the many.
Could there be somebody who would give her heart to you?
Or but a part of it?
Or even cast a glance at you?
The least of these, I do believe
is what I'm likely to receive.
Happiness, what can that be? . . .
My heart is thirsting so . . .
I could drink a deluge, yet
one single drop of dew may never fall on me!

Contend not with thy fate, good man.
Bear hardship with serenity;
Bring happiness to others, if you can.
And though unhappy, you remain,
be the ground where grows the grain,
for others to come reaping;
Be a lamp, which burning bright,
does spend itself,
that others may have light."

Destiny, of ill or good, brought an occasion when
the dear girl was to meet with him,
as in a room, they stood.
Throughout the meeting, time had sped,
and there was very little said.
But after that, they were to meet quite frequently.
Whether by design or chance?
This, the girl nor young man knew,
but to spin the moments longer,
more communicative grew,
though as yet,
they had not spoken of themselves,
since first they met.

There came a time however, when he opened up his heart.
(By persuasion of the maiden, or of himself I cannot say.)
And the story of his life was then narrated.
He spoke of how alone he was.
How as a child, there was not one whom he could trust,
but for himself, had he to fend.
Not one had acted like a brother,
nor had one become a friend.
All he could recall, he now related.

How in truth, it was a thief had found him in the street.
When forsaken, he was taken by a beggar-woman.
And later was he brought up like a slave.
He stole, he begged, he served in bondage . . .
thus from infancy to manhood.
He spoke about the squalidness
which had oppressed his childhood.
And of that more acute distress,
the crushing of his spirit, when a youth.

Looking back upon his life,
was to look into the abyss,
from which he had ascended, grip by grip.
There lay suffering and heartache,
like the seething black flood-waters
of a mountain lake:
His spirit reeled,
as from his eyes, the tears fell
like blood upon a battle-field.
And the girl wept too.

PART THIRTEEN

Starkly different was the scene,
between Silvester and the maiden's father.
He was summoned one day, by the pompous lord,
and harshly reprimanded,
for making rebels of the serfs,
by leading them astray;
Her father had concluded,
should he persist in such behaviour,
he would be dismissed.

With dignity, the youth replied, "My lord,
I must question your exhortation,

For I am past the age of school,
though neither was I used to such, when there.
If my crime is incitation,
sentence me according to the rule.
If I am guiltless, by what right am I reproved?
And regarding my dismissal,
resorting to intimidation,
does not frighten me.
As much could I earn anywhere, anyhow,
as that, I am living on now.
But I'll not go from here, because here, I feel to be of use.
And you, by your discharge of me, should not tempt me to.
Not with your own interest at heart,
for either will come the whole village with me,
or you'll be the one to depart . . .
Do not take this as a threat, but rather as good counsel.
I know the tenants well.
I know how much they love me.
And what, though without my intention,
could be done regardlessly."
So spake the youth.
He made his bow perfunctorily, and left.

The following Sunday, a sermon was preached against Silvester.
Unto the congregation, had the priest spoken with horror,
of how he was an atheist,
and agitator!
If tolerating this man even further,
for their associating with a rebel,
amid two worlds, would they be lost.
He could incite them into murdering the King.
And friends of an atheist, were after death forbidden
to enter into Heaven.

Set right the situation, ere disaster came upon them,
and the final reckoning.
The priest exhorted them, with tears within his eyes,
to consider earthly happiness, and that of paradise,
lest death be chosen, and damnation,
instead of life, and sweet salvation.

Aroused into anger,
the people now rushed from the church,
(that house of God, and serenity,)
and like wild beasts, ran to the youth,
whom yesterday they had called Father,
to banish him from the vicinity:
If he, by the morrow, was seen to remain,
he would be instantly slain.
The youth was to reason as much as he could,
he never had spoken so well.
But in vain.
Wherever the priest was to raise up his voice,
Truth could be twisted and crucified,
until there on that spot, Truth had died.
The priest was inspired by a devil.
The devil had no greater power over God,
but his language was more influential.
For to gain an advantage, God cannot use guile. –
With curses, and menaces, the people deserted the youth.

For a moment, his spirits were shattered.
He was oppressed by hopelessness.
Thoughts gathered overhead,
like a flock of carrion-crows
descending on the dead.

"This far back, are people!" was his despairing cry.
"This far back, are these I love,
whom I live for, and would die!
Still as they were a million years ago . . .
But not, not in a million years should this be so;
They are in childhood, easy to fool, and easily led.
And therefore do they need support,
as from the child, the man doth grow.
I have no cause to be surprised.
Priests and Kings, those earthly gods,
have kept the people blind, since ancient times,
in their desire to rule,
for only the blind can be tyrannized.
Poor wretched people, I pity ye.
Until now have I fought for thee,
but henceforth shall I fight
with double might!"

Came the eventide. Came night.
It was to be his last spent here.
Within a tree-lined avenue, he stood among the shadows,
gazing upward at the window of the manor,
where the maiden, gazing outward, should appear.
But this was now deserted.
No flower adorned the balustrade,
no maiden was in sight.
Yet steadfastly did he abide,
as though he were an effigy,
looking upward from the grave,
like a spirit, petrified;
The silent grief, in face so pale,
was covered by a moonlight veil.

Once more, he felt her tiny hand was held by his, and yet . . .
how strangely unaware he was of touching her
when first they met . . .
And as he turned around to go,
he saw the one he sought above,
standing by his side below.

"I was waiting," said the youth,
"to see you at your window.
I waited in the hope that I would see you one more time.
My goodbyes, to send to you, before I leave forever,
by dumbly speaking to you, with my eyes.
But now my voice can speak instead.
I pray good fortune may be thine, beyond all expectation.
And with my words, now this dear hand,
can into mine be taken.
God be with you, my beloved.
Only you, in all the world has ever named me as a friend,
and I have you alone, a friend to call.
I have no keepsake ere we part.
You, yourself shall stand within my heart,
as in a hovel, does the icon on the wall,
which the wretched resident, every evening at prayer,
is on his knees before;
Had my heart treasured memories,
most glorious to own,
I would cast them all from me,
to have you there alone.
God be with you! . . .
When you receive report of me, if good, believe
the reason is
that worthy I may be of thee.
Never would I bring you shame,
or cause you ever to regret that you befriended me.

Indeed, I hope to make your proud
of the friendship you allowed.
God be with you, guardian angel of my soul!"

The youth prepared to leave,
but the maiden caught his hand,
impulsively impelling him to stay,
trying to speak, yet losing her voice,
eventually, haltingly to say:

"God be with thee . . . Go . . . Go . . .
God be with thee, most noble youth!
Could I but leave with you also, I would do so willingly.
Bright star of mine,
are you now dropping from my sky?
Are we ne'er to meet again?
I love thee.
This, I must confess,
ere my soul erupt from me,
like the molten stone of Vesuvius.
I cannot be thine, yet I love thee!
But I swear, by God's Holy Mother,
that if I cannot be thy wife,
I shall not wed another!
Take this ring . . . this betrothal ring . . .
Rend the diamond from its setting,
rather than my loyalty.
God be with thee . . . God be with thee,
Sweet dream of my life!"

Heaven overcame the youth.
He sank beneath such bliss.
Upon his knees, unto the girl
he clung, her knees to kiss.

Leaving the village, the following day,
hundreds of times along the way,
he was to look at the ring.
Only then could he be sure,
that what occurred the night before,
was not the foolish fantasy of a fevered dream,
but an actual happening.

The road he took,
(the reason why? He could not tell,)
was to the capital,
where in the past,
he stole, and begged, and was a menial.
On the outskirts of town,
he rented a small attic.
And there within,
he knew not what to do,
or where begin.
A sudden knock assailed the door.
'Twas opened for a lady veiled . . .
She stepped into the room, and now
upheld the veil above her brow . . .
in silence, standing motionless . . .
Assembling his chaotic thoughts . . .
he looked upon his loved one.

"I followed you," the maiden said . . .
"But if I burden thee,
and you tell me to depart,
I shall not return.
I will sit upon thy step, until I break my heart.
I followed you. I could not stay.
I was behind you the whole of the way.

And now that I am here with thee,
what shall you do with me?"

The youth replied without a word.
He drew her to his breast.
They clung together, weeping happily.

"You'll not send me away?" she said.
"With you, I can remain? . . . .
I'll give you all my happiness,
to share but half thy pain!
Together, hardship and distress,
with you, I would endure.
And if that once, I should complain,
ne'er believe, I'll love thee less
than e'er I had before!"

PART FOURTEEN

They lived together, as man and wife.
No priest had bound them to each other,
but God and Love.
No vows of loyalty were made,
such words had never passed their lips.
Of that, within their hearts, they knew without communication.
And like the very stars above,
which vapid breath cannot attain,
they yet unsullied, did remain.

The days were sped by happiness,
Months passed them aside . . .
when the world was unaware of their existence,
and they were as oblivious
of the world outside.

But finally, there came a day,
when sharply to the youth, his spirit was to say:
"Awake, awake,
'twas not for thy sake, you were born,
but for the others!
Have you forgotten your vocation?
Arouse thyself, prepare to work!"
And even more sharply was said to the girl,
by the voice of Domestication:
"To work, arise, immediately,
for otherwise, the two of you to starve today,
tomorrow, will be three."

Silvester set to work. He began to write.
As inspired by the spirit, he compiled a manuscript
worthy of his honesty and powerful insight.
He took it to a publisher,
and when the manuscript was read,
this reply, the publisher unto Silvester said:

"Sir, you are a great man.
Yet also, a great simpleton!
You are great, for this is a masterpiece.
Better than this,
not even Rousseau has written;
But you're foolish because you imagine
this work can be put into print.
Have you not heard of censorship? . . . .
Well shall I tell you now?
It is the devil's thresher,
we must keep the sheaves below,
the grains of truth to thresh from them,
the naked stalks to throw unto the public,

that upon these, may they ponder.
If you wish this work in its entirety,
the thresher, to get by,
for every seed, seen to remain,
a leaden bullet would I gain.
And not the grain, but thorns would grow,
to over-run and stultify.
If you do not believe my words,
why you, yourself may try.
And for it too, thy pay receive."

The youth returned as though
his head were dazed against a wall.
He sat up to the table,
assuming to be able
to write with such a sweetness,
and so innocuously,
that upon it, would the censor's hand fall lightly,
sliding over, as on velvet.
Yet when the work was finished,
he observed that it was more unreservedly outspoken,
and contained a bitterness
greater than before.
Ten times, a hundred times, he wrote it all anew,
and then tore up the pages, every time he read them
through.
He was bound to keep returning
to the same familiar lines,
for he found that nothing other, could he do.
He finally decided, of that which could be printed,
there was nothing in it anyone could learn.
Yet what he could express to give enlightenment,
would never reach the press.

"It's soul-destroying," he gave cry.
"Is there no way for my words to be made known?
My spirit has a living fire, which could alight the world,
must it be smothered in me, 'till I myself expire?
And meanwhile, I must live . . .
On what, to live am I?
Must I disavow my principles,
and righteousness deny?
Am I to side with villains, the deceivers of mankind?
No, by god, no!
Rather die of hunger and end my life in squalor,
than begin again to steal and beg,
and be subdued in servitude.
Each letter of that literature
which had not issued from my spirit,
would be a forgery of my signature!
Unto God, my thoughts, you are captives
about to be walled in alive.
My head is thy prison and coffin . . .
Oh but no, you cannot die so;
For surely, the day must arrive
when the door of your prison will open.
Throughout the world then in your streams,
circulating warmth within light, ye shall go
as freely as summer's sunbeams!"

Thus calming his thoughts,
the youth laid them aside,
to cultivate others,
the bread to provide.
'Twas hard, perhaps harder
than the work he began
wood-cutting from morning
until eventide.

And often late into the night,
he was to see the lamp-light die,
ere he could sleep as deeply.
Yet after so much work, the table
even then stood bare, as often
as were frost-ferns
painted on the windows
by the white cold winter.
And tears stood frozen in the maiden's eyes . . .
But the warmth of her feelings
were never to freeze,
throughout the passing years;

The family of three
had soon increased to four.
And fourfold was the misery
within that tiny attic,
where the walls
were streaked by rains,
and bore embellishments of mould.
Where three were sleeping in one bed,
two children with their mother.
And at the foot,
upon the floor,
there lay the man,
upon baled straw . . .

And now,
the first ray of sunlight
is cast upon the brow of the sleeping man.
A golden garland thus presented
with God's salutary kiss!

PART FIFTEEN

The family awaken, one by one.
Firstly, the husband,
though the last to fall asleep.
Secondly the mother,
then their little son . . .
And the babe?
Not yet awakening,
but peacefully sleeping . . . .

The parents and the little brother,
stepping with soft tread,
whisper to each other,
scheming not to drive the dreaming
from the infant on the bed.
Good brother, good parents,
why bother step quietly,
inaudibly whispering so?
Shout out. Stamp about.
Make a din . . . do not fear,
it would not awaken the baby,
the clamouring, it could not hear.
The baby is dead!

What could the mother be feeling,
when she saw that her baby had died of hunger?
What of the parent whose hunger that day,
had taken her darling infant away,
a cherubim infant babe?

Were the power of God's right hand transfused into my own,
could I express her suffering?

How a thousand claws had rent the heart of the poor
woman?
Leave her be,
Leave her cast over the body,
to cry, to cry, to cry.
Crying out from the depths of the abyss,
unto Heaven, in her pain,
cries which clawed the face of God,
mud-spattering His spirit! . . . .
Leave Him be.
Leave Him be.
In His torment,
trouble not the Almighty.

Standing before the tiny corpse,
the man was dumb with sorrow, or,
who knows, perhaps with joy?
With joy to see him now at peace,
his death, as merciful release.

The little boy stared fixedly
at his baby brother,
puzzled by his pallidness,
why so white and motionless,
and wond'ring, if that he were dead,
whether he was hungry? –

Slowly, but slowly to pass were the hours,
one, after another.
In her grief for the dead child, the mother
was losing consciousness.
With lighter heart, her spirit's wrath
subsided into ease.
The froth of lamentations

no longer stormed the heavens,
but gently shook like ears of corn
stirred by a passing breeze.
The corpse, she cradled on her lap,
to rock from side to side,
half-singing, softly whispering,
like the forest's murmurings
of autumn leaves at eventide:

"Sleep, my little son,
what is your dream?
Tell it to me.
'Tis beautiful isn't it,
that which you see?
You do not sleep yet 'neath the face of the earth,
your mother shall rock thee.
'Tis your mothers embrace,
thy mother who's nursing thee.–
Sleep, sleep my pretty one.
White sunbeam, white flower,
black earth to devour.–
The sky's red from blushing,
kissed now by dusk;
Thy face I am kissing,
yet this does not redden.
Why is it not flushing?
Smile but once upon thy mother,
precious little one! –
Green mound . . .
White cross . . . .
Thou below ground . . .
I above . . . .
What's dropping upon thee?

Not the rain, but my tears.
Be quiet, ye acacia leaves,
be silent in the cemetery,
I am speaking with my child.
Such lovely things we're saying,
you must listen. –
Is your head not aching?
Is your little heart not breaking?
Is the earth not heavy
which upon you now shall rest?
Whose embrace was kindest,
that of mine, or of the coffin?
Sleep, sleep,
my little white dove.
Goodnight, but I beg thee:
Keep dreaming about me,
that we are together, my love."

As the dead child was lulled into sleep
by the mother while she herself dreaming,
the father was deep within thought as to how
could he purchase a coffin,
and pay for grave-digging?
Not even a farthing lay in his possession.
He raised his eyes to scan the room,
in search of something that might sell . . .
but there was nothing. Nothing!

What thought is this, upon which he doth linger,
yet obviously further distressed?
He noticed the ring,
her ring on his finger,
the most valuable thing he possessed . . . .

Must he sell this,
so that into the earth,
the child would not go naked?
Must he, from his most precious keepsake, be parted?
Through so many sorrows,
for so many years,
it had never been wrest from his finger.
Must he finally part with it now?
The worry of this, was to turn his hair grey . . . .
Yet for him, there was no other way!
When drawing the ring from his finger,
he felt that his heart was torn out by the roots . . .
His past fell apart from the present.
The bridge had collapsed, which connected
his springtime and winter.
The ladder ascending to Heaven
had crashed into pieces.
Yet that all this should happen,
he readily accepted,
so that into the earth,
the child would not go naked.

The babe was buried nicely,
laid in a silken shroud,
within a coffin made of hardwood.
A marble stone, the grave displayed.
The ring had fetched a princely sum,
and all the burial fees were paid . . . .
The man took nothing for himself,
save a solitary mite.
And taking heed of their great need,
he set aside a sum for bread.
And yet of this, with every bite,

the instilled poison should have killed him,
but life, it was to give,
for he still had long to live!

PART SIXTEEN

His thoughts were told they must not die,
and that a day would dawn
when they would leave their prison,
to go out into the world.
And so it was.

What for so many years, he had struggled to suppress,
because of all the efforts made in vain,
at a time of opportunity
was reproduced again.
A private printer, he had traced
in a secret hiding based below the ground.
Here, were printed all his manuscripts.
And what did these contain?
That the priests were not men,
but devils.
That the kings were not gods,
but men.
And that all men are equal.
Man not only has his rights,
but unto his creator, he also has the duty
to retain liberty.
For he without value of God's divine gift,
unto God, shall of no value be!

A book was published.
Throughout the world, it had speedily spread
as if it were carried by lightning.

The people were thirstily swallowing greedily
the crystal clear drink
by which they were refreshed.
But those in authority,
furrowing their foreheads,
and whitening with anger
were thundering emphatically:

"This book is seditious.
It violates religion,
the author must be punished,
according to the law!"
And the terror-stricken people,
said heatedly, repeatedly:
"This book is seditious.
It violates religion,
the author must be punished,
according to the law,
the law which is infallible!"
And the author had to pay the penalty.

He was taken captive in the middle of the street.
And as they were dragging him away,
"Stop. Oh stop. For pity's sake!" the prisoner did entreat.
"I am not not trying to escape.
I'll peacefully go where you will,
but wait for just a little while.
See yonder window, 'tis my room,
in which my wife and child do dwell.
Take me there, but for one moment,
that once more, I may embrace them,
and of them, take my farewell.
Then I'll not cause you any trouble,

when arrested, I'll not grieve.
But otherwise, I shall not leave.
Rather would I
having said my Goodbye,
go to Hell, than to Heaven
without a farewell.
Are you not husbands and fathers?
What would you say,
how would you feel
if others dealt with you this way?
I have no-one in the world other than my wife and son.
And they have no-one in the world but me, no-one;
Let me pass, good men.
Let me pass, that we may see each other
yet once more, perhaps 'tis for the very last time.
Have mercy not on me, but them.
Believe they are innocent, and should not be made to suffer.
'Tis not for the law to kill them, nor thee! . . . .
Oh God, if by words, they are not to be moved,
they should, by my tears, be touched now . . .
these drops of blood, in beads of sweat
which are upon my brow! . . . ."

On bended knees,
like that happy time when he had clung to his beloved,
both arms around his captors knees, were flung.
But he was now raised brutally.
Mid gibes and vulgar laughter, he was carried shoulder high,
and taken to a cart for his conveyance, which stood nearby.
And when he saw that gentle discourse was to be of no avail,
he was overcome by anger.

Summoning all his physical strength,
he now endeavoured to escape by means of force.
With the courage of a lion,
and the strength of the insane,
he grappled, fought and struggled,
but in vain!
Overpowered, and tightly bound,
he was thrust into the cart,
from where he roared at those around,
like some wild animal:

"My curses upon thee, and all thy descendants,
ye devils in clothing of human skin,
deep layered with Satanic linings.
Replacing the heart, you have pulsating toads!
Cover thy faces, with superating sores,
as thickly as depravity is laid upon thy spirit.
And satiate your appetites, by eating up the worms
of a maggot-ridden dung-heap!
My curses on thee, and thy kings,
in whose name can Virtue be lead to slaughter!
So too, I curse you, tyrannical King,
thyself, reckoning to be God.
A demon you are. Demonical Falsehood! . . . .
Who has entrusted the sheep to the wolves?
Your hands are as red as thy scarlet robes,
your face is as white as thy crown.
Your heart, as black as the mourning-clothes worn
long after your deeds,
like the long shades of night
drawn from dusk until dawn.
How much longer will you be usurping thy authority,

with stolen power, by stolen rights?
Like the ocean, your subjects will rise up against thee.
And though you be defended by
a million of thy mercenaries,
God forbid that you should die
within the fight there valiantly, as would befit a man:
Thou art a fly,
and cowardly, shall be the first in flight.
You will run off to hide, beneath thy throne,
like a terrified cur scuttling under the bed
to be routed from there, amid guttural cries
of laughter a-sputt'ring into thy beseeching eyes.
You'll be licking the feet of old women and children,
and those who were once kissing thine,
as they will be kicking out all of thy teeth,
a-grinning before thee, in line.
Steadfastly thus, shall thy unworthy life
be kicked from thy body!
Then be thou cast in the slough of despair,
such as that I am lost within now! . . . .
Oh my son . . . Oh my wife . . . ."

PART SEVENTEEN

Whether he had been asleep,
and this was the awakening,
or having lost his wits, was he
returning to sanity?
Was it but an hour or so
since first he was beside himself,
or was it several months ago?
Somehow, Silvester could not tell.
He lay in silence wondering,

wondering what had taken place,
and what with him, was happening now?
He looked around, but nought could see,
so dark it was, 'twas dark as Hell.

At last unto himself he said:
"It is indeed, the night.
I slept and dreamed continuously.
It is but vague within my head,
and yet the dream was full of dread.
I was speaking to my wife,
and yet it seemed she could not hear,
nor could I arouse her, when I tried.
Though never could the night have been
as drear as this awakening.
Are you asleep, my love?
Are you asleep, my dear? . . .
You surely must be fast asleep, for you have not replied.
Sleep my loved ones,
sleep in sweet tranquility.
Yet still not dawn?
Oh when will morning be?
The density of the dark night
is suffocating me!
Awaken Daybreak,
lift thy face,
bright countenance with smiling lips,
or do but show thy finger-tips. . .
My head is splitting.
It burns as though a blaze within,
and fire is spitting through my skin.
Soon to burst will be my brain! . . ."
He raised a hand to wipe his brow . . . .

Oh what clatter echoed now! . . . .
Upon him rattled a heavy chain.

As reality returned again,
waves of coldness swept through him
like rushing winds amidst a ruin.
With horrifying clarity, he remembered everything . . . .
He had been arrested in the centre of the street,
and by force was dragged away.
He could not see his wife and son,
nor could he speak with them.
No farewell had taken place,
no parting glance into those eyes
wherein his joys and riches lay!
And now, 'mid prison walls was he,
who knows how deeply underground?
Deeper than sunken corpses
rotting 'neath the cemetery!
Whenever would he see again, the light of day?
Whenever would he see again, his dear beloved ones?
Perhaps never!
Whyever was he cast into this dungeon of damnation?
He knew that he had only done what God had given him to do –
and that was for the common good of everyone.
Advocating everybody should be treated equally,
this common good was freedom!
And yet to try
to take the mote out of another's eye,
was to commit a mortal sin.
For who-so would be liberated,
must then be exterminated!

"Holy Liberty, how I am suffering for thee!"
the captive cried, aware of spreading pain.
"Though if I am to stand alone,
as I have stood within the world, the many years before,
I'll sit upon this granite floor as proudly as a king
in the possession of his throne,
as happy now to bear this chain,
as once I was to wear my ring!
But what of my wife . . . and what of my son . . . .
What will become of them without me?
Who will support them?
How shall they be fed?
Who is to nourish them with love and bread?
And what will become of me, now without them?
My heart, how you ache.
If not made of stone,
why do you not break!"

He cried, he groaned, he raved deliriously,
eyed unceasingly by Darkness,
regarding him unblinkingly,
'til slowly he was silenced.
Exhausted, he surrendered to submissiveness,
remaining dumb and motionless,
impassive as the stone on which he sat,
and his blanketing of darkness.
Thinking came now without feeling.
Softly down, his thought came flutt'ring,
like a bird on broken wing:

"My prison,
ye coffin of my fellow-men,
who built your walls?

Who will batter them down?
How much longer will you endure standing alone?
How long have you stood?
Who was last sitting here, on this cold stone?
One such as I, a martyr, to die
for his conscientious belief?
Or a thief?
Had he mouldered into dust, within this place of horror?
Or does he see again God's lovely world?
The fields. And flowers. Stars and trees.
The mountains and the plains . . . .
Perhaps I'll nevermore see these,
or by the time I do,
'twill be so late, I'll not recall their names . . . .
Am I sentenced to one year,
when to remain one moment here is an eternity?
Time trudges
like an aged crippled beggar
haltingly, upon two crutches . . .
For one whole year?
One year or ten?
A score perhaps, or more?
Arise, ye dead. Come unto me.
All ye, who ever suffered here.
Let us converse a little while.
Teach me how to spend the time.
Rise up, ye dead, and come . . .
Perhaps I am already dead?
And do but dream within my grave . . .
a fearful dream . . . .
I am dead, yet buried here alive . . . .
I am dead . . . .
My heart shall beat no more . . . .

This throb that I can feel must be
the last convulsive tremors
of my sick etheric body."

Silvester finally stopped thinking.
Not a thought, nor an emotion
occupied his heart or head.
He sat there like a statue,
as unblinking as the night,
as it crammed into the prison.

His limbs grew numb,
and he began to lose all consciousness.
His head, so pendulously hung,
his body, tumbling, over-swung,
until he fell upon the stones . . . .
lying lengthways, within sleep,
or was it deep unconsciousness?

He lay there a long time, without any movement.
But, possibly for the want of air,
and as if he was fired by gunpowder
or scorched by a branding iron,
he suddenly leapt to his feet.
And calling out with such despair,
his voice rang so heart-piercingly,
that the cold walls immediately took up his cry,
repeating as desperately,
"Hold on . . . Hold on!"

Thus for a long long while, he stood
with arms extended, hands outspread,
'til these, by slow degrees, descended.

Sinking down into his place,
sitting back against the wall,
his head bowed low upon his chest,
and two great tears, from two great eyes
began to fall.

And now as if his soul cried out,
was uttered brokenly:
"Couldn't stay . . .
Gone from here . . .
Leaving me . . .
'Tis over!"

What possessed him?
Who was leaving?
What was over? . . .
Merely dreaming?

'Twas no fantasy . . . .
Though stranger is reality!
When lying there upon the stones,
close beside him appeared a lady
whom he realised was his wife.
She stooped to whisper in his ear:
"God be with thee, I am dying."
She kissed the man upon his face.
At this, he jumped unto his feet . . .
Opening his eyes,
within a second he had seen his dear beloved.
In the prison there was light.
But as she disappeared from sight,
darkness then returned again
like midnight after lightning.

"God be with thee, I am dying!"
he repeated harshly.
"This I heard in that sweet voice,
which nevermore am I to hear:
God be with thee, I am dying . . . .
And God be with thee, Leaves of my spirit,
stripped as I am, now you're taken from me;
Yet when you were taken, then why was I left?
What reach, what reach has a leafless tree?
Where can it be swept by the storm?
Withering so, how can I find thee,
that my life's remains,
unto thine, can blow? . . . .
I have no further need of life. All purpose I have lost;
You were my reason for staying alive.
It was for you, and in you, that I could survive.
My love-goddess, you were my sole reality.
As for the rest? humanity, liberty?
These now are empty words for me,
mere illusions, fantasies,
for which none but the foolish strive.
You were my sole reality, my love-goddess!
Yet I have lost thee forever!
If I could burrow through the earth
like a mole, I would not find thee . . . .
Dust is to become of me, like that of any other,
the same as all the rest, and no better.
And even in dust, thine own shall intermingle,
as if but of a plant, or animal.
I cannot bear this loss, the burden is too great,
while beneath it , I shall break.
If only I had said goodbye.
If only I had said to her one single little word . . . .

Nor had God allowed me this.
And now it is all over. 'Tis all over.
How cruel God is!
How foolish the man, to bow down before Him,
in worship of this missing Father! . . . .
Thou tyrant God, I curse thee!
Remote, on thy celestial throne,
you sit in such cold dignity,
like tyrants here on earth who reign,
Thou art as apathetical.
And yet accursed God, thou art even more tyrannical.
The Sunrays of the dawn, each day,
you dip in the blood of the broken-hearted,
to paint your tarnished ragged throne
in scarlet shades, re-started
over and over and over again!
As you deny me,
So shall I deny Thee . .
You shall have one servant less.
Take back this life, like alms-giving thrown down to me.
Take it back, and dole it out to another.
Let someone else exist on it,
I'll not live on such charity.
My life, I throw before Thee now.
Break it into pieces like a useless pot!"

Thus shouted the prisoner,
so frightening the darkness,
that by its trembling, all shuddered therein.
Thus had he shouted, ere he was to fall,
from violently crashing his head to the wall.
From this dreadful blow, the wall had then resounded
as though itself had suffered the pain.–

There lay the prisoner with blood-covered head.
But he lay, unconscious,
not dead!
His life had become so increasingly hard,
it was now unto him, as unbreakable
as his spirit was unto the anguish,
as his prison was unto the dark.

PART EIGHTEEN

It is ten years, since first he sat amid those prison walls!
Ten years at liberty without, would still be long,
let alone spent within
that infernal pit! . . . .
His hair and beard had wildly grown,
and many times he peered to see if it were turning white?
But always this appeared to be yet still as black as ebony,
for naturally above the dark, colour did not show.
Although it was already white,
White as a dove.

Ten years had passed, ten years amassed
as one long endless night,
of waiting, watching for the dawning,
wondering, when would come the morning.

Occasionally, he fancied that
more than a century had elapsed,
more than a thousand years since he
was cast into this prison.
And how it could be for the world,
the day of judgement was now over.
All Earthly structures had collapsed,

except this one existing place,
where he remained
forgotten.

All passion died within his heart
No more at God, he swore.
No thought came into his mind of God nor man.
He found that even Sorrow died,
and only sometimes softly cried,
when from a dream awakening.
For within dreams, that lovely vision seen before,
the wraith of his beloved,
came many times to visit him.
So faithful, that she came to him, yet from beyond the grave!
But upon awakening,
directly she had disappeared,
then softly had the prisoner cried.

But why did he not see his son?
Unto him was brought but one;
Why could not the eldest come?
He told himself the answer to this question:
"My son must surely be alive, for he does not appear.
Only thou, my love, my cherub,
only the dead can enter here!
My son therefore, must be alive.
And probably, since long grown-up,
is thriving now.
I wonder what became of thee,
my little orphan, my poor son? . . . .
Who knows?
If taken by necessity, a robber you could be,
and the hangman is to bury thee . . . .

But if you are to follow in the footsteps of your father,
and now, like he, live underneath the ground,
perhaps you lie within this very prison.
Why, you could be so close to me,
that you could be my neighbour?
My son, my son, do you remember me?
Art though remembering thy father lovingly?"

But hush, what stirred?
What unusual sounds were heard!
The prisoner, straining to attention,
evaporated into silence, daring not to breathe.
His spirit, so long tightly shut,
was opening up unto these sounds,
like a flower's cup to the sun.
And breaking now into a smile,
it was the first upon his lips,
since the latter ten long years had first begun!

Upon a window-ledge nearby,
perched high upon the prison wall,
a little bird was sweetly singing,
sweetly singing, giving call.
And oh, the sweetness of that song!
Silvester said, or rather thought
from daring not to speak lest he
should drive his visitor away:
"Oh God, what joy, what ecstasy!
'Tis the first time that I've heard such tones as these,
since being here,
even though I've been here for so long.
Sing, Sing my little bird,
sing to me your song.

SING, SING MY LITTLE BIRD,
SING THY MELODY.
YOUR SONG IS SO EVOCATIVE,
IT'S BRINGING BACK TO ME
THAT I WAS LIVING LONG AGO,
THAT EVEN NOW, I LIVE.
YOUR REFRAIN REMINDS ME OF
MY LONG DEPARTED YOUTH.
THAT TIME OF SPRING,
AND THAT SPRING-TIME
OF SWEETLY FLOWERING LOVE!
YOUR SONG AROUSES MY EMOTIONS,
YET IS SOOTHING SIMULTANEOUSLY.
PERHAPS UNTO MY SUFFERING
THE CONSOLATION WHICH YOU BRING,
IS EVEN SWEETER THAN THE JOY.
SING, MY LITTLE BIRD, SING! . . . . .
But who sent you unto me?
Why soar unto this wall so high,
where nought but curses fly? . . . .
Great heavens, I guess you are trying to kill me,
you are to kill me by happiness! . . .
Yet something else is telling me
that soon I will be free.
That while I am in this vile place,
I am not to die,
but out there in the open air,
below God's lovely sky . . . .
Little bird upon the wall,
thou art the world's free wanderer,
the herald of my liberty! -

I have no doubt that this is so.
Be strong, my heart,

If not yet broken from my sorrow,
break not from my joy.
Verily, this is to be.
Tired and sickening of shame,
the world is coming to an end,
and is about to fall.
But firstly must be opened all the doors of the entombed.
And the first of happy tears to flow,
shall be upon the faces
of all who suffered here for freedom.
Thou art heralding my liberty,
little bird upon the wall!"

A key rasped in the prison lock.
The startled bird took fright.
The prison guard pulled back the door,
and said unto the captive:
"You're free."

Crying out in sheer delight, he put his hands unto his head
as if to keep his wits therein,
from trying to take leave of him.
"This hasn't flown away from me,"
with childish gaiety, he said:
"I have it here, my thoughts are clear,
I haven't lost my head . . . .
I'm aware of what is happening.
I know that I am free . . . .
So therefore are the people.
And the country, it is free?"

"Fool," had sullenly the guard replied:
"Why care about the country?

Be satisfied that you are free."

But not a word the prisoner heard.
By then, his mind was far away . . .
Already half within the world,
he sought the grave,
in which his dear beloved lay.
"Firstly, I must go to thee,
to thee, my soul departed.
And this my quest, to kiss the earth wherein you rest! . . . .
What ages am I here restrained,
while from my hands and legs
are hammered now these chains.
These few moments seem to last
longer than when forcing
through the long years of the past!"

PART NINETEEN

Like mother's milk unto the child,
as hungrily and sweetly drawn
was taken now the air.
And with each single breath he drew,
unladen from his spirit, was exhaled
one bitter year.

Light, and like a butterfly,
he felt himself to be.
Flitter hither, flitting thither,
here and there haphazardly,
inhaling Nature's newly-flowering

memories of days gone by.
Invigorated by the air,
his spirit leapt, rejuvinated.
But his body, feeble, aged,
still remained emaciated.
He walked slowly without ease,
limping, leaning on a stick.
His long white hair, and long white beard
flowing, blowing in the breeze,
flapped about distractedly!
The past ten years were unto him,
as living through one hundred.

Arriving at the house
where he once lived within the attic,
the people stared appraisingly,
but he met no acquaintances.
Unless they had forgotten him
perhaps the residents were new,
for he could not remember them.
He asked of all the tenants:
Do you recall that family, who lived within the attic?
The family now living long above?
And this was asked repeatedly
of members of their families.

" Oh indeed, I do remember,"
cried an aged goodly woman.
"Poor young wife. A lovely person.
Such a good soul too, she was . . . .
But the husband, godless devil,
he was punished, so they said.
He was taken off to prison,

off to prison, he was taken,
and is still there if not dead.
When his wife knew he was captured,
never to be seen again,
could not bear her life without him,
died heart-broken of the pain.
I can't conceive how this could be,
that it was possible to love,
that it was possible to die,
over such a man as he!"

Silvester heard this conversation, without showing an emotion,
as if he were not the one
of whom she had just spoken.
"Where is the young woman buried?" he asked:
"And what became of the son?"

"Of what happened to the son?
Well that I wouldn't know.
I never saw the little lad, after the burial.
I don't know what became of him,
nor where they buried the young woman . . . .
I wasn't at the burial,
to that, I didn't go.
Though I dearly would have gone,
– but for my religion."

At this, unto himself, said he,
"I will find her. Now I'll find her,
outside of the cemetery.
All the graves upon that ground,
I will see, until she's found."

And trudging to the cemetery,
the graves he looked at, one by one.
And when he came unto the last,
the round again, he had begun.
But still he found not his beloved.
Why nothing, nothing now remained!
The heavenly being had left that place,
disappearing like a sunray,
without leaving any trace!
The wooden marker, long uprooted by the storms,
was batted down,
And the mound, completely flattened by the rains.
She was with God! . . .

The poor old fellow was distraught,
that he ne'er found the grave he sought.
Of the tears which had remained
throughout his years of misery,
none were to fall upon the earth above his dear beloved . . . .
But he drew comfort from the thought
that this must be life's final blow.
That with all joy, was taken too,
for ever, further sorrow.
And so, into the world, went he,
hollow-eyed, and vacantly,
like a soul-departed body,
disembodied, like a shadow.

He was ne'ertheless mistaken.
This was not his final grief.
When he asked ere leaving prison;
"And the country, it is free?"
he had not waited for the answer,
having stated his belief.

And very soon was realised
his country and the people were now more greatly tyrannized
then even when ten years ago,
Silvester had protested;
"The growth of tyranny, day by day,
diminishes human dignity."
So was his suffering in vain?
The sacrifice, for nothing?
What use were idealistic hearts unto humanity?
And yet must every effort fail?
Are struggles all, of no avail?
Impossible!
This I shall cry, though I but try
one hundred times again!

Upon this thought,
the fire within re-kindled into flame.
And flaring unto his bowed head,
the enfeebled aged man, an energetic youth became.
A daring plan, his brow concealed.
On his resolution, could possibly hang
the fate of the nation, or even the world.
This plan was far from new.
Thousands before had thought of it too.
But supposing that someone could carry it through?
And supposing that he were the one? . . . .
His secret schemes of ways and means,
were kept unto himself.
And he was careful not to sleep near others,
lest he spoke within his dreams, and
his strivings came to nought, ere came the light of day.
Neither would he rally comrades,
for the awesome task in hand.

He chose to act upon his own,
to see it through, as he had planned,
not from vain desire for glory,
but that should the plan miscarry,
the danger, would be his alone. –

The city lies steeped within clamour and light.
Thousands of people are rushing in unison,
gushing along like a river.
Into the streets, they are crushing and pushing,
their raucous cries ringing,
"Hurray, Hurray,"
faces and clothing of brightest array,
for today is a public holiday!

What is this day of celebration?
Perhaps God is come unto the land,
to live in HIS own image,
And to give with his own hand
unto the people within bondage,
their long lost liberty;
that there should be such light, such jubilation!

Nay; This is not God.
'Tis another comes this way,
so much the more inferior,
he thinks his is superior.
The King! . . . .
Aloof, among the people, nose wrinkling into frown,
like a mastiff amid puny curs,
disdainfully, he looks around.
And everywhere he turns to stare,
knees and heads are sinking down,

undulating like the rushes,
when the wind blows o'er the marshes.

Now the hordes of slaves are shouting,
lungs about to burst:
"Long live the King!"
Amid those thousands upon thousands,
who dared not to call out this?
Or durst to cry out other? . . . .
Dare anyone? . . . . One dares . . . .
But one among the many . . .
Another cry, so loud 'twas heard
above the uproar of the crowd,
had rent the air proclaiming:
"Death to the King!"
A fire-arm exploded,
the King, so proud,
collapsed in a heap, within mire.

Cowardly tyrant, get up off the ground.
You'll surely not find the gun there in thy clothes,
nor in thy heart, shall the bullet be found.
Thou art unhurt.
Thy life is preserved, having sold yourself unto the devil.
Cowardly tyrant, get up off the ground!
And brush from thy image, the dirt.

Who is the assassin? Who is it? Where is he?
See him there standing . . .
but now he is lying,
already half-dying.
Be glad that he is old,
for you can spit upon his face.

You can kick his broken body,
and the white hairs on his head.
Wretched, wretched people,
yet more vile, one-hundred-fold!
Why incite the curse of God?
Are you not satisfied?
Is not that enough, which doth already lie upon you?
Was it not enough, that Christ was crucified?
Accursed, wretched people! Why?
So every Saviour of the World,
are you to crucify?

A few days later,
there was raised a scaffold in the Square.
An aged man went up unto his execution.
And as the executioner,
with his bright sword, for dark of death,
beside him was to tread,
the aged man, until the last,
had looked upon the mob.
In riotous rows, they assembled about him,
maliciously gloating. And savagely shouting
as in his eye trembled a tear of regret.
He was now sorry
for those who had kicked him,
for they who were looking on with such delight,
at seeing him dead . . . .
Swiftly the sword had flashed,
swiftly, so swiftly,
sending horrifically rolling
the head . . . .
And the people cried out simultaneously:

"Long live the King!"
When the corpse was removed
by the executioner's men,
Silvester was buried
beside a gallows-tree.

PART TWENTY

Since the death of The Apostle,
rose a new generation,
whose faces were to redden
upon mention of the fathers.
And because they desired to do better than those,
they became better people,
for all they required was the will! . . . .
This new generation had bravely revolted.
And that which was inherited was bequeathed unto
the fathers,
the chains which cast them down.
The fetters broken from their hands,
upon the sepulchres were thrown,
that startled by the clattering cacaphony proclaimed,
were those also within the earth to be
ashamed! . . . .
The Great Ones were commemorated,
who, in service for the free,
had preached the word of Liberty,
and yet, as their reward,
met shameful death! . . . .
In remembrance of their victories,
memorials to these heroes bore their venerated names
interwoven like a wreath.

And the people would have taken them to
consecrated ground,
where they should have lain in honour,
but where could they be found?
Within the dust of long ago,
beside a gallows-tree!

THE END